ARIEL YELEN

I Was Working

POEMS

PRINCETON UNIVERSITY PRESS

Princeton & Oxford

Published by Princeton University Press
41 William Street, Princeton, New Jersey 08540
99 Banbury Road, Oxford OX2 6JX

press.princeton.edu

Library of Congress Cataloging-in-Publication Data

Names: Yelen, Ariel, author.
Title: I was working: poems / Ariel Yelen.
Description: Princeton: Princeton University Press, 2024. | Series: Princeton series of contemporary poets
Identifiers: LCCN 2024012583 (print) | LCCN 2024012584 (ebook) | ISBN 9780691264066 (paperback) | ISBN 9780691264073 (hardback) | ISBN 9780691264080 (ebook)
Subjects: LCGFT: Poetry.
Classification: LCC PS3625.E436 I33 2024 (print) | LCC PS3625.E436 (ebook) | DDC 811/.6—dc23/eng/20240327
LC record available at https://lccn.loc.gov/2024012583
LC ebook record available at https://lccn.loc.gov/2024012584

British Library Cataloging-in-Publication Data is available

Editorial: Anne Savarese and James Collier
Production Editorial: Theresa Liu
Text and Cover Design: Pamela L. Schnitter
Production: Lauren Reese
Publicity: Jodi Price and Carmen Jimenez
Copyeditor: Jodi Beder

Jacket illustration by Jack Reynolds

This book has been composed in Garamond Premier Pro

10 9 8 7 6 5 4 3 2 1

CONTENTS

I.

I Was Working

My second job was waiting in a window
behind the window of the job I was on

the clock for. My third job was scheduled
for that evening, but not yet

confirmed. My fourth freelance job wasn't active
per se, but I was actively

pursuing clients. After much consideration or
to be more precise, after being forced to act

on what I'd been denying for many years
(and the feeling of finally

acting was like a breath
of air and the air very much

like the vacuum left
when a train rides next to then

past you on the subway
platform), I decided to quit

everything but work. I quit my friends and quit
living with the human I shared a life with, for I

was about to quit everything we shared. My meals
became quick, I stopped seeing

a therapist. That perfectly abstract
yet persistent weight on my body and psyche at last

let up. It rained. Information became
fluid. Smooth. I could now fully take on

the professionalized work that somehow generated
getting and doing more professionalized

work, which was the only way out
of the perfectly abstract yet persistent

weight. It wasn't the more jobs I had
the more money I made. It was

the more jobs I had, the more
I could work. I didn't have to answer

to a therapist about why no pleasure. I could
have no pleasure, and work. No one needed

me because I quit everyone, so
my attention could always be split in four

places at once—my first job, my second, my
third, my fourth. At any point a fifth

would come along, automatically multiplying
as they tended to. When I did arrive home, the human I once shared

a life with wasn't there to say, I'm so happy
to see you. No one was happy to see me, and so

at last I could work. No one said it's okay. It wasn't
okay, thus my work flourished. And though

they once loved me, no one
reached me. Meanwhile, new

platforms continued
to make themselves available

I'm depressed to only now have discovered

This great poet
Imagine if I'd discovered her earlier, I'd be rich
Oh! the poems I would not have written, inspired
By reading her
Had I read her earlier, I would've thought *this*
Is it—and the desire to write
Would drain from my body
In service of us all
And I would move on
To making money
To acting, maybe
Or farming
Or simply to being of use in some other
Less painful way

Poets Need So Much

Eruption needs bigger sound
Binding contracts need soothing
Brick needs breath
Walls need asses
Muscle needs flab
My hands are flagging cabs
They need holding
Through visions
Of butter-colored daffodils
The poet wants money
The problem is she's thinking

Revolution

The new microwave at work has begun
To make the most beautiful sound as it finishes cooking
When it first appeared some weeks ago it was impressively silent
While heating food on its circular base
Either someone changed a setting or it has liberated itself
I've begun singing the alto part in harmony with it when it plays
And I've been adding a note, the minor third
Before dropping to the lower fifth
To finish the song in unison
Music under most circumstances
Will take desperate
Measures to come back into your life

Five blocks and three hours away

The view from the office so stunning it's propaganda
Character named "I" makes a face like wow
We talk about nothing, tensely
Over a technically
Continental breakfast
As it turns out trauma's what we all have in common
But is anyone here worried about the fact that I'm an artist?
I grant you permission to love this glistening city
But first it's time to sit down and write about the thing you always
    write about
While structured desire makes paragraphs of your poems
You write even though there are facts out there
That should inspire you to focus on nothing but deleting
Nothing but changing your name
Nothing but closing your bank account and joining a militia
This is the glitch I hope to figure
Out how to live with

What Devastates Me Is Me

A small
Militarized form of life
Spending time on a Stairmaster
Walking uphill
For an ass

This poem stabs one's own eye

Leaving me to see only the fruit I'm allergic to
Truth sets you free, I text you
You text me
I text you

Almost to first and saint mark's
Green apple blossom tightly wound
Little pink buds abide
Tomorrow you congratulate your co-worker on her new job

Meanwhile you feel as though you've been stabbed in the heart
Not by her leaving, but by heartburn from chipotle
You may as well have used a sick day
You ride busses

B61 is true
M103 is true
They turn in their true and extreme ways
But seriously congratulations

The problem with beauty is that it convinces me of achievement

Really it's just that time has passed, what was green
Is now orange
This poem compares the seasons

And philosophizes beauty in the form of strands
I think I owe my boss a hello
I think I owe him a turkey sandwich

First I'll dive into excel
Where the cells welcome my touch
I check the boxes, it's classic, it's plain

Life really does make people into poets
Kind of pervy not to be a poet or artist if you think about it
Standing around drinking but what will you make of it?

The contradictions of my life ward off robotic becoming
I think they're worth it
Let's at least agree that being turned into a marble statue

Is the goal of our labors
I make some interesting progress and follow up
Thanks for your email, now you can sign off my child

But be careful not to lubricate the truth
Let beauty commute you

This poem says yes

I like to write it while someone takes me seriously
Little do they know I'm writing the story of our conversation
    in my mind
In plain speech, nothing frivolous or flowery
No commentary, just details like

Then she said, and then I said, and then
She said, "the soup is actually good"

As I write, my cubicle is being cut in half but I can go home early
That time is finite is the announcement of your life

Note the screensaver, how it displays the unlikely story
Of a peaceful transition
From pristine glacial lake to arid red desert
Meet you at Rainbow Falafel in thirty

Taking the ferry to work like an adventurer

Like I'm a Viking white-collar worker
Wonder why the dean wants to meet with us in a small group

Hold on let me get my jacket
No one at work can know I have breasts

This poem forgets to float
The money's that good

Remotely, I see you
Have a lot going on

From your home office we hear
A truck beep loudly over you while you speak

I wonder who's prayer
It's answering

Prayer for tax season

May I meet
the dean's corporate tactics
with the powerful hush
of a weeping

willow, May I work and
be paid despite
poor ergonomics
and poor
economic policy

May I pay my taxes
with the ease of one thousand
cherry blossoms raining

down, May publicity efforts
fail to show us the truth,
leaving us to figure it out

The shoulders of poets
hurt. May the future stay
fertile. The past is gone

All morning, tax evasion

In the subway station liquid
Drops on our heads
While the F train never comes
Trash overflows
Outside the marble university

Utopia's attainable but pressing
On truth where it's tender
Results in feeling metal
Bands around your heart snap open
It's pretty hardcore

This poem's about the kind of neglect
Writing can't solve
No amount of fragments will do
Only being more disgusting
Give me something brutal for lunch
Like escargot or liquor

A Poetics of Nothing

Do you know if you can buy a hole?
We could treat the hole with care

Clean it out when it grows
Full of dust and stuff

I've been told the edge is near
We could practice falling

Or create jobs
Purchasing and selling holes for a little

More than we earned for digging them
To potential hole-buyers we would say

Holes are great for looking into
Shout into a hole and a hole

Swallows your shout
How wonderful they are for seeing through

Burying something
Dangling your leg

I see us performing our shtick
Where while you dig the hole

I stand outside of it looking in
So that while we talk to each other

Your voice gets farther
And farther away

And farther
The hole-buyers will ask what good

What good is this
What use?

I don't need more things to avoid
I don't need more things

For dangling my leg in
To pull myself out of

To fill
Shout at

Trip over
Consume me

What are you selling me here
This good-for-nothing *nothing*

(The *nothing* punctuated
By an echo from the hole)

We would say stop yelling
This is our job

Holes are good to have
We insist

Reincarnation

What's rising up like wheat, like corn
in July, inside me
I'm hospitable to, out
of habit. Opening my mouth
to share what will inevitably outgrow me, minding
its blood-red
root as it's passed around and consumed
easily. The nature of inadequacy-
shaped desire:
classed, distorted, cramped.
I may as well desire feces
which I can't help
but produce in movements, affording
me a certain lightness no money could
but that's a lie. Yet I remain hospitable,
wedding it to my person such that it becomes my personality,
such that it becomes mythology
of twenty-first century life, that we desire
such things and are such and
such way

New Year Poem with Green Flooding

The mechanics of how one
Lives life
Astound me, and yet
They're all I've ever known
I don't want the job
Of hating my job
I want to flood things with love
Like the green flooding in
I'm a lamb
I'm a lion
Seduced by my senses
Funded by morals and despair
I trip out on time
On the dumb sun
Some days are long days
Punctuated by meals
By anchovies
By cornichons
By mustard
Dear god, by mustard I write you
Someone was holding my hand
We searched for fancy
Mushrooms in the cemetery
All I've ever wanted is to be
Someone's chanterelle
Mom, everything's gold
Dad, the sun's here but in the trees
Jo, the overripe persimmon's fainted
Open on the cutting board
The new ancient year begins at sundown
The drama

Bodies and Signs in Time

To be able to sink into my appreciation for your body, I first
must evaluate the way in which I do, to ensure through a series
of checks and balances that my appreciation will appreciate.

What I mean is, to be able to love each other requires that we not
stay together in physical space, but rather disappear
from one another daily to construct a kind of something
that allows us to, in free time, love each other.

This creation casts a curfew, but we must keep building, or nothing
will be built. Or is it that we'll have built a nothing, which law
and language don't acknowledge.

With things as they are, we only know what we'd do without
the constant building. Or is it that we only do what we can in the air
pockets where it's not (which isn't much if you've fantasized
about what we might do without it).

Possibly, though, the two states of being might've merged—our
dreams taking the form of the negative space,

our wildest imaginings vast
landscapes populated

with infinity big and strong somethings to live by

II.

IN FREE TIME

Thank goodness people
Come here and thank god
They leave at some point
Praise be there's a seat
Oh no it's taken
Great it's open now
Scrolling through the news
But my phone screen stops
Picking up my thumb
News of death and war
Everywhere except
A couple places

Shell of a person
With fixed gaze on clock
Eats robotically
Language of things on
Repeat while people
Try to say feeling
The right not to be
Exposed to what's new
Ads and some info
The bike rack casts a
Shadow, tattoos a
Snake onto pavement

Mine eyes are spicy
From the screen, my knees
Are sore from sprinting
In platforms across
The city to all
My things, everyone
On the train's yawning
I try not to, fun
But it starts to build
Back in my throat in-
Side my ears it wants
To stretch the back head
Open and take breath
In—like a baby
Trying not to cry
The worker must yawn

When you're sad it is
A relief to point
Cursor on corner
Of cell then drag it
Right, light up the page
Of little white bricks
With a square that says
These boxes will live
Be copied, pasted
Echo in excel
While others will fade
Into abstraction

It's okay I eat
My lunch on the bus
It isn't tuna
It is hard-boiled egg
With scallions and dill
Please don't look over
As if I'm evil
Accept the chaos
Of other people

The philosopher
Wonders what it is
What is love they ask
To know what something
Is is to name what
Something was back when
X was pain Y was
Pleasure and Z was
Just something I said

I consider the
Bed made when I have
Hidden the mattress
Now it is summer
I bring twenty books
With me to my desk
Open only one
Eat a leftover
Salami sandwich
While talking on phone
After I tell you
Something, I tell you
I meant what I said

The QR-code works
If you get pretty
Close to it, zoom in
Move your oils around
The screen and then click
The menu's too big
I'll just have water
And an eggplant parm

Bunch of hot babes in
Leather jackets ride
Ferry to work, me
Included, my hat
Flies off and away
Deserve it, I'm late
Plus prayed for some breeze
While running, captain
Yells from up high "clock
Waits for nobody!"
I smile 'cause I know

Held the door for her
Then had to go right
Back out the same door
He held the door for
Me then I used my
Key to go back out
Bought a tunafish
Sandwich and chips, lunch
Is served! At my desk!

Wind blew so hard it
Pulled the umbrella
Out of its socket
The weekend is gone
Waves mucky and big
They scared me, forecast
Said rain, it was sun

I cook oatmeal but
Burn it quickly, dump
Rice milk in, voilà!
Remembering when
I ate mint ice cream
Last night under tin
I don't have the time
To think about this
Revelation or
Is it just caffeine?
To be determined

Now that you've given
Birth things are diff'rent
I'm no longer scared
You will float away
At least not today
Check my phone to see
Boss sent an email

Paper stacks cover
Books I'd like to read
I put the stacks there
To hide them from work
Also to hide them
From myself, the fear
Of finding the truth
While in cubicle
The printer blinks red
Wants my attention

Multiple people
Have provided me
With information
Regarding the fact
That the soup today
Is actually good
But I am against
I'm against the soup

III.

What Is This Air Changing, This Warm Aura, These Threads of Air Vibrating Rows of People

This small effort
Because this little singing
This little sound
Small song
This fathomless effort
This voice which comes from the gut
This soft effort at making song
This effort at song
This effort to make song which birds do effortlessly
What birds do effortlessly
This tiny bird
This tender worthy effort
And sometimes it is no effort
No effort to sing
Sometimes I've had a drink or two
Sometimes it's effortless to make song
If enough people sing in a group
If I'm part of that group, I cry
I'm holding a thing that breathes and makes sound
Where song comes from and goes to

Poem Toward People

I've always been obsessed with people—
whether or not I know them. Obsessed
by our knowledge of each other, the quality

of connection, our friendship or non-friendship,
its relation to other connections. Obsessed
by the way a new connection can change pre-existing

ones, reorder them, renew them, fine-tune
or disappear them. By the light pressure
of an other's existence, which in turn grows

me. Obsessed by memory and lack of memory
for the way things were—I don't think I'd recognize
you if I saw you on the street, though in the past

so obsessed I thought almost everyone
was you. Obsessed with leaving people
so I can obsess about them again.

By thinking with and through people, dead
and alive, without whom I'd be a different person,
think different thoughts. Even obsessed

with the version of me I don't know, walking around
having met different people, thinking different
thoughts, moving in a different direction, away

from people and toward the self,
or the desert, or the sea, or the god, or the page, or the mountain,
or the canyon, or the forest, or the dark

The Dynamic of Moving a Tree Stump

A group of us meet in a field to move a stump
Someone brings gloves and hands them out to everyone

Someone says beautiful stump
The person who needs the stump moved says

Ya, it's beautiful right
Someone else asks, what is this, cedar

No one answers
Someone finally says, looks like it

But the stump has become its own thing
It doesn't seem to be part of the tree family anymore

It belongs to heavy, oversized objects
Group projects

Things that must be moved
Conversations about trees

The person who needs the stump moved says
It might be easier if we roll it

We roll the stump to the truck
Okay lift

Okay hold on let me get the roots
Okay you can go to that side

Okay watch out
Move away

Be careful
After we move the stump to the truck

It turns out there's another place we need to move the stump to
Some people drive in the truck

To where the stump needs to go
Others walk

Some of us become committed to getting the stump
To its final and proper place

Some of us become less useful

I miss the feeling of being free
and connecting the dots

Like the whole world was conspiring to show me myself all along
While running out to get kebab on 23rd
If you go through the floppy discs of my life, you'll find files of good
Questions next to files of confusing outfits, unrequited love
I was unafraid to have and then a shift to never again
You'll find some hardcore theoretical work being developed
Then forgotten due to drugs
The archives show attempts to make
Poetry above all else
And time wasted looking at pictures of people
And wondering about relativity
This poem boils love down
I'll just eat it at my desk
Bad theories of mind inside folders of awe
The push to know
The push against knowing
You were weeping freely at the foot of the source
I saw you of course
And I saw you at the water fountain, thinking
That to ensure smooth operations, fire the conflicted self
Luckily they accept venmo

The Small Picture

There once was a person who could only see
the small picture. Even when they breastfed
as a baby, all they saw was breast, all they heard
was mother's voice. Now, as they walk
through the park, their friend exclaims *it's a beautiful day!*
But all they see is their dear friend's face soften
into a smile. When this person has sex, they see only
a wilderness of hair. When others allude
to their wealth, flaunt their clothes or properties,
all this person sees is pixelated fuzz
dangling off a cashmere sweater, the cement bottom
of a saltwater pool, the sharp edge of the kelly green
logo on a website meant for banking

Blood-Clock in Hancock, New York

Blood clock of January, you're ticking
Ritual and bandaged, you bind
My friend texts a picture of persimmons
to which I respond *permissions!*
'Cause a robot doesn't know what fruit is
All robots wonder is *am I allowed*

How will the robots translate our Art
History of blood: dogs ripping a hog apart
on a snow just like this snow. On a day just
like this day—a January day. An elemental day

When my blood-clock first started
I thought war was a thing to learn
from a book. I thought by now a robot
would know fruit when it sees it, could taste
a peach and say, *pick it!* And that the Delaware
River would be bigger than this

I assumed ticking was a myth
I thought time was a carousel
I was already riding. Now I'm
bleeding on the snow, ticking like the hog

Everything good? Yes. Everything?

Yes, thank you, everything is good
The day is good
The sweater I wear, good
The weather is perfect
The book I'm reading, good
My walk here, good
And good is good!
Who can say otherwise?
Who can complain?
What's all the angst?
The coffee's strong, no?
The sun out, right?
My walk here pleasant
How bad could it be
A cloud in the sky?
A scale of one to ten?
You have it good, no?
How bad is it really
How bad is bad?
Everyone suffers?
And what's a person anyways?
How long do they last?
Do machines break?
I want to believe they do
The wi-fi stops working all the time, so I know they do
I hear brand new teslas malfunction
The dishwasher in the apartment I'm renting leaks
The Titanic sank
Remote controls for TVs rarely work to begin with
The elevator in the library's down all the time

Our subaru broke down while dropping me off at the airport
Rain breaks the credit card system at the grocery store
I have to pay with cash
The levee breaks
Sprinklers fail to put out fires
Tractors often need fixing
Planes crash
The vending machine breaks, pop-tart gets stuck
A windmill's blade falls off
My phone overheats and turns off
Apparently, the torsion catapult breaks
When its counterweight is too heavy
Cannons fail if there's a fracture in the wall of the cannon tube
Civilizations break down
I visit their crumbled sites for proof
Broken stone and marble
In a guarded field of mint
Wild dogs bark nearby
Empires fall
And famous warmongers go down, they do
First they might murder their own daughter
Near two rivers, under a plane tree
While the oppressive sun beats down
But do you see that new cement factory
And beyond it the horizon line of the mountain, where
There now stand three wind turbines
(Sure to break someday)?
That's where even the deadly
Sun goes down, it does

Red Star

If it's true I look so familiar
As you say, exactly like someone
Then why not the birds

Why not the familiar birds
On their branch
With the same-as-it's-ever-been rain

Drizzling from the sky
Why not proclaim to know
These things from somewhere
If it needs to be from somewhere

And to swear you know them
From your life during which light
Became evidence of rain
In the next hour or so

And by now you basically know everyone
Familiar as we are to one another
Born as usual

As ever, suckers under a red star
So familiar it's everywhere

In every face or phrase, may as well
Swear to know the soil too

Could it be all those years lived
Memory fails
And yet there's something
About the ground

I'd Rather Be Love-Low Than Money-Low

When you're love-low
You might look down
At the grass. Wonder how
Do I start fresh. Thinking in green
You'll realize you're money-low,
A job will do

When you're money-low
You might look down at the grass
Wonder how do I get the gig
Of just growing. Thinking in height
You'll realize you're love-low—
That it's all trampled, the grass

Tide's Out (of Money)

Rosehip invested, violet from spending
Maroon-washed seagrass capitalizing
They say the dollar's Seagullian in thought
They say barnacled but good investment
Blistering cost, hedging salty dolphins
Another sun-dappled account balance
Washed up on shore, we can take advantage
We can make the most of the crab market
Sea's willing to trade its somber aura
Apparently, I look bloated with cash
I'm still moon-heavy with expenses though
To make some money, I painted canvas
I painted a picture of speckled stocks
Look, low tide's a late bloomer but worth it
Come now, it's time to invest the seashells

The time is now to invest in seashells
The troops need them for splashing in tide pools
Babies squish seaweed for sea-wide sanction
Breeze-blowing philosophies of defense
Theories of exporting the dune grasses
Sand and scrubby pine-caused casualties
Ocean flooding veiny trails made by drones
As seaweed clings to a beautiful bomb
Anchored deep in the encampment is what
At first glance looks like some fish enemies
But is algae posing as a missile
Pretending to be a windy blockade
Made to look just like resistance seafoam
For the purpose of fighting for the bay

We must fight for the right to use the bay!
1–800 what are you waiting for?
Doors are opening for the lobster-snapped!
800-PAIN-LAW rains down from a cloud!
Passion meets crusted-shell-purpose dot com!
Groceries in minutes! Down at the pier!
Lifetime trial of smashed crab seagull food!
You deserve free shrimp dot com hashtag shrimp!
Join now! YOU can swim with US! Sink with us!
When every nap is bottom of the sea!
Try mental healthcare for the ocean floor!
Try cloud-hung mist essential spray for hers!
Try tsunami for hers, become a wall!
Try becoming a wave, roll up, wash out!

Become a wave, spend your savings on it
Go into debt for the pull of the tide
Tide's out (of money) but worth it they say
Taking out a mortgage to finance crab
If you're the sea you can take out a loan
Pay your interest with what starfish remain
Refinance to flood the renovation
The Atlantic owes the Pacific now
Meanwhile the Pacific owes the Black Sea
That's why the rocks on the Cape are for sale
Why soil and sand and grass and saltwater
And why the tide pools are full of champagne
That's why inflation by the seaside's high
That's why the driftwood's looking to sublet

The driftwood's looking to buy us some time
Digging the trenches so couples can wed
Drilling the sand so that flags can fly high
Mass casualties of fishhooks and rope
Mass shipments of salted water for fun
Bombardment by the jetty for sunset
A poverty of good sense by the bay
A deal struck between seagull officials
Nothing will be done as the tide comes in
Floating ducks quacking bombs on enemies
Some patriotic fish becoming spies
Some purple-washed tint on the horizon
Warning the navy their wetsuits won't work
Armies coming into port riding sharks

Save big on the small shark-riding army
No money down! No beach! And no interest!
Do you own an oyster? Wanna save big?
Want the real briny real beauty special?
Wake up the beached whale for the new year's sale!
Get the jellyfish holiday ready!
Bargain with local clam communities!
Bargain basement for sandy promises!
Save five percent with basin bonanza!
Save the optimized shimmering lighthouse!
Save ten percent on menswear for mussels!
Save one bird dollar on spending two now!
Save fifteen percent on saving the sea!
Cockle-crusted e-sale bobbing lightly!

Cockle-crusted e-sale bobbing slightly
E-commerce-strangled cash cows on the shore
Don't swim by them, they'll scorch you with credit
Just float on your back through the ATM
Just float on your back through the index fund
Try to ride the wave of pearly profit
The sun's burning through an insurance claim
Is it true what floats in the bay's fair game?
And are whitecaps getting minimum wage?
Are harbor seals signaling fish to trade?
Is the junk bond junkiest when anchored?
Are the delicate deposits ebbing?
Are the wetland's grassy assets lending?
Rosehip invested, violet from spending?

Underwater Theater Show

We're living longer

but we're more afraid—

fear of
fear

in our blood now

plastic insulation sparkles in a window

afternoon sharpens
geometric brick design

it's my landlord's birthday

Erotics of Being a Self

Your dreams growing in length

The length of which is your life

Full of symbols and questions, you wander unresolved

Attached to ideas of the self

That maintain ideas of the self, you bring this self to others

You ask them to hold it, to care for it

You ask, Can you watch it? Can you feed it?

Do you like it?

You ask, Can you make it go away?

Big Future has always surrounded the self

But is not enough to keep it

Death is the body sensing something more interesting

Wrestling with narrative drives tears down cheeks

And the tears flow into the streets where people need to shop
It's not practical
We can't ride boats everywhere, this isn't Venice
It's New York City, baby
This is an office
Today's my birthday
Across the room is a revolutionary
Placing donuts on a tray
Putting pink roses in a vase
You see, mine's a revolutionary
And rose-adjacent life
The cake's dairy-free
Let me cut you a piece

Carrying It

Living with others, and sensing
them—and though determined not to invent
what it is they're thinking and feeling—
knowing based on lived experience
that something is not right, and to feel that not-
rightness, to walk around
with the weight of it, knowing
that some are skilled at not carrying it, but added to that
there's the weight of knowing
you may be wrong, that it's possible
you're carrying something
for no reason, but that to put it down
would be to change your life

ACKNOWLEDGMENTS

Many have had a hand in the creation of this book.

Thank you to the editors, guest editors, and staff where versions of these poems first appeared: *The American Poetry Review, BOAAT, BOMB Magazine online, The Brooklyn Rail, Changes Review,* The Poetry Project's *Footnotes, Nomaterialism, Pigeon Pages, Poetry Magazine, Prelude, Second Factory, Social Text, Tiding House, and Washington Square Review;* and to *Spiral Editions* for reprinting "Revolution" as a limited-edition broadside.

Immense gratitude to Rowan Ricardo Phillips for selecting this book, for your guidance, deep attention, and care. To Anne Savarese, Julia Haav, Sydney Bartlett, Jodi Beder, Jodi Price, James Collier, Theresa Liu, Bob Bettendorf, and everyone else at Princeton for your crucial work. Thank you to Jack Reynolds for drawing the perfect clocks for the cover.

To my teachers, to whom I will always and happily be indebted, thank you. To Sara Jane Stoner for creating several magical spaces to write into; multiple poems from this book were written in their glow. Thank you to Ted Rees for facilitating two workshops that shaped much of this book and for your meaningful feedback. Deep thanks to Rutgers–Newark MFA faculty Brenda Shaughnessy, Cathy Park Hong, Rigoberto González, A. Van Jordan, Jim Goodman, and Rachel Hadas.

Thank you to the brilliant women of Cadosia. Many thanks to Daisy Atterbury, Alex Cuff, Alina Pleskova, Ryan Skrabalak, Irene Silt, Susannah Simpson, Liz Peters, Dan Poppick, Emily Caris, Ricardo Hernandez, Như Xuân Nguyễn, Grey Vild, and Stacy Szymaszek for either offering feedback on the book at various stages or writing alongside me as I wrote it. Deepest thanks to Phoebe Glick, Emily Lee Luan, and Tracy Fuad for your careful readings of this book, your support, and your poetry. Thank you to several dear friends who, over the years, have asked to read my poetry, and laughed or commiserated with me about various jobs, New York, and the creative life; you've kept me afloat. Gratitude to my family for your steadfast encouragement.

Finally, thank you Evan, for always being first reader, but mostly for your love and all it makes possible.

www.ingramcontent.com/pod-product-compliance
Lightning Source LLC
Jackson TN
JSHW020028141224
75386JS00027B/747

I Was Working

PRINCETON SERIES OF CONTEMPORARY POETS

Rowan Ricardo Phillips, *series editor*

For other titles in the Princeton Series of Contemporary Poets, see the end of this volume.